I0554185

Funny Food Stories

by

Dolores Maria Davis

Copyright

© June 2022

Dolores Maria Davis

All rights reserved. Except as permitted under the
U.S. Copyright Act of 1976, no part of this
publication may be reproduced, distributed, or
transmitted in any form or by any means, or stored
in a database or retrieval system, without the prior
written permission of the publisher or author.

Genre: Memoir/Cookbook

Cover Design by Quincy Macklin

ISBN: 978-0-9976240-4-5

Printed in the United States of America

Dedication 5
Funny Food Stories 7

~ For Rex and Nikki Ringer ~

Funny Food Stories

Grandmother Carmen

Carmen Sanchez del la Ortiz, my paternal grandmother, entered this world on a ship off the shores of Costa Rica in the late eighteen-hundreds. Imagine her mother, Antonia, delivering her baby in that environment. The family had boarded a steamer in San Juan, Puerto Rico, to escape the Spanish American War. With no Panama Canal yet built, they rounded Cape Horn at Chile's Tierra del Fuego to make the long sail up the coast of South and Central America.

When I met that grandmother, the ringlets of her red hair were beginning to turn silver. Her tight skin glowed like a ripe nectarine. She paraded her squat build, narrow shoulders, and hippy posterior with authority. Her fiery temperament and lively manner could cause problems, yet

Grandma Carmen was kind and friendly with me. I think it was because I was fair, like her. In Hispanic families, the fair are always revered.

Whenever I climbed the stairs to her large Victorian house, I would be greeted with delicious food smells and a spotless interior.

"Soy en la cocina," she would call, and to me, that meant we were about to eat food that influenced me more than I knew.

Her warm kitchen often smelled of simmering Spanish rice, with hints of chili. The ceiling seemed so high, and the yellow walls gleamed. A small stack of logs sat next to her wood burning stove. Each time we visited, she proudly told us she chopped the wood herself. I knew of no other grandmother who did this.

When the giant cast iron stovetop grew hot enough to satisfy her, Grandma began her tortilla making, but not before she would cap all the openings on the stove top to make a flat surface. There, she would cook one large flour tortilla. After kneading the dough - made from white flour, a little lard, water, and salt - she formed a ball about the size of a grapefruit. The shiny round would be covered with a tea towel made from a flour sack. There it would sit for about twenty minutes. Then the magic would begin. Talking effusively, she slapped the dough onto her large round oak table using a little flour to keep it from sticking. From one hand to the other, she patted it until she had a thin tortilla that went from the tips of her fingers to her upper arms. Each time Grandma would toss the tortilla from one arm to the other, she critically examined it for thinness. When the tortilla was opaque, she threw it on top of the iron stovetop where it bubbled.

At this point she would say, "There is no Indian in me, I make flour tortillas, not corn. We're Puerto Rican!"

Carmen's mother, my great-grandmother, Antonia Ortiz de la Pena, stood nearby but like a shadow. It was Carmen who filled the room, both with spirit and importance. Great-grandma Antonia was short, dark complexioned, and diminutive. She resembled the Caribe Indians pictured in a National Geographic magazine I saw years later. But so proud was my Grandmother Carmen to be white, she simply ignored the Indian characteristics of her mother Antonia.

When the tortilla came off the heat Grandma folded it in half and then in quarters. She tossed the triangle onto the center of her round oak table that she had covered with a hand-embroidered cloth; the communal bread from which we all tore pieces, for our fabulous lunch.

My Spanish Rice

Since I was ten years old, I remember my grandmother making this rice, and I am not sure this is a replica, but the taste is very close.

Ingredients

1 cup short grain rice
olive oil for sautéing the rice
2 cups of chicken broth
4 cloves of garlic
1 small tomato coarsely chopped
1 tablespoon oregano
t teaspoon salt

1. Sauté rice in olive oil until it is a light golden color (very important).

2. Have ready and pureed: garlic tomato, oregano, and salt, using a little chicken broth to blend.

3.   Add the puree to the hot golden rice, then add the broth. Simmer uncovered until done, about 15 minutes.

Note: The rice must be golden as it has then puffed and will absorb much more flavor. Pureeing the garlic-tomato mixture is the equivalent of using a pestle and mortar.

Pitiful Alice

Alice was new to the neighborhood, and nobody liked her. Her thick glasses were held together in the middle with tape, her ten-year-old voice was nasal, and her dishwater blonde hair (as we used to call it) was stringy and oily. I felt sorry for her and tried to incorporate her into our games. The other kids didn't like that idea, but Alice was grateful that I had accepted her. One day she asked me to stay over at her house for the night, but not for dinner.

The landlord felt sorry for Alice and her mother, so he rented them an addition to his garage for a few months. Single mothers were an anomaly in the late forties. I really didn't want to go there for the night and discussed it with Mother. She said they were a sad pair and didn't need to be rejected, but if I went and felt uncomfortable, to call her and she would come and get me.

When I arrived, Alice was in bed and her mother was in a rocker. Alice invited me to get under the covers with her. He mother had prepared something I had never eaten before. It was white bread spread with margarine and sprinkled with sugar. Above her mother's chair were several classic books, a whisky bottle, and a small glass. Her mother filled the glass with the liquor and drank it. Then she lit a candle and took a book from the shelf to settle in her rocker.

With gleaming eyes, Alice whispered, "My mother is going to read to us now." I remember chewing the white bread and the crunch of the white sugar as we listened to her mother's lyrical voice reading a chapter from Little Women. I also remember that her mother slept in the chair all night.

Sweet Quesadillas

I made this Mexican equivalent and served it with Mexican chocolate as a special treat for my kids.

Ingredients

6 corn tortillas

Jack or Muenster cheese (although I prefer Havarti as it mimics a Mexican cheese)

brown sugar

1.   Simply make quesadillas in a skillet with a little oil, and to the cheese, add about ½ teaspoon of brown sugar.

Note: Tortillas warm well wrapped in a towel in your microwave to make them pliable. A spray of vegetable oil added to your skillet is ideal for using minimal oil in making your quesadillas.

The Reynolds Family

The Reynolds family house was two doors down from mine and intriguing to my ten years. I fantasized it as a grand Spanish- styled mansion you might see in a Hollywood movie. Looking back, I realize it was a modest white stucco built in the 1920's with a red tile roof.

Summer evenings, I watched Mrs. Reynolds, her husband, and mother-in-law sipping cocktails on their porch. "Cocktails" was a word other neighbors didn't use. The family relaxed on a colorful, striped canvas swing, while their radio played classical music. Mr. Reynolds called the covered porch a "portico." Their grassy front lawn was shaded by Mission fig trees with snarled, serpentine roots.

In late summer Mrs. Reynolds let neighborhood kids climb the trees and pick baskets of ripe figs. My mother always made lots of fig jam. I hated it.

The Reynold's house was crammed with musical instruments and exotic furniture. Sometimes Mrs. Reynolds would call to me and say, "Dolores, would you like to play one the of pianos?" She meant the pump or the electric.

I always chose the pump, sat down, put my feet on the pedals and played Moonlight on the Ganges. The invitation often came with sugar-coated jelly donuts from the Helms Bakery truck, sometimes fresh, sometimes not.

Occasionally, Mrs. Reynolds would reach for her violin and accompany me when I wasn't pedaling too furiously. She also played a heavenly-looking harp that sat in the corner of the living room. In another corner stood a scary Chinese couch, with carved dragons for arms. The eyes of the dragons were inlaid with abalone shells and looked evil. The couch stood on a dirty Chinese rug. Mrs. Reynolds never cleaned anything.

Black Chinese pajamas were her daily attire and never covered by an apron like other mothers wore. Most days, she painted her lips with fuchsia-colored lipstick into a perfect rectangle, just like the movie star, Joan Crawford. I couldn't wait to grow up and dress like that. I saw women in movie magazines with haircuts like hers. It was called pageboy style. The color was like the darkest red crayon in my coloring box.

The kitchen sink held a mountain of dirty dishes. The family ate a lot of cheese and crackers, canned foods, and pastries from the Helms Bakery truck. Because Mrs. Reynolds didn't like cooking, she stored hundreds of canned goods. I have a vivid memory of her bent over one of their record players listening to Caruso singing Ave Maria while spooning beans from the pan she had warmed them in.

A wide arch from their living room led to a dining table where a French horn reached to the chandelier. Violin cases, a trombone, two or three ukuleles and a couple of harmonicas, a concertina, a banjo, and a dusty accordion crowded the dining table too. It was the first time I saw and got to shake a tambourine.

The Reynolds' son Peter played the drums. He was allowed to take off his closet doors, and cram his large drum set into the enclosure. Guitars, trombones, and trumpets leaned against his bedroom walls.

One afternoon, Peter sat on the curb eating an applesauce cake. Mrs. Reynolds said, "Oh look, Peter is eating a cake from the bakery truck. I won't have to fix dinner for him. Mother Reynolds and I can get an early start to the opera."

The family liked to boast that their garage stored 7,000 records and 5,000 piano rolls. Late in the afternoon Mr. Reynolds, who wore a big felt hat, would turn into their driveway in his pea-green 1939 Packard sedan. His car was the longest in the neighborhood with a huge wheel attached to the side. When he drove into their driveway, he turned the motor off, coasted to a stop, and got as close as he could to the garage door before stepping on the brake pedal. Mr. Reynolds was big and round, so after opening the car door, he just slid off his car seat, not bothering to use the running board as a step. He would head for his worn overstuffed giraffe chair and plop into it. Beside it sat his Victrola record player that had a crank and a horn. He cranked the player and sat close to the horn, then lit a cigar. Sometimes he arrived with a big white bag of fried chicken for his dinner.

On special evenings, Mrs. Reynolds and her mother-in-law allowed themselves an evening out. They dressed in black velvet clothes, pinned with antique platinum jewelry, and wrapped themselves in tattered furs. They donned identically styled, burgundy-colored wigs and their faces were painted up like a couple of old harlots, some unkind neighbors used to say. They were on their way to the red car, several blocks away, that would take them into the city to their beloved opera, for their real sustenance.

My Unorthodox Fig Chutney

I grew to love figs and today have a tree of my own. They tend to arrive in great quantities, so I make chutney. I'm not sure how authentic this is, but I often share the condiment with my Indian friends, and they approve.

Ingredients

12 figs, halved with top of stem removed
1 large onion, sliced thinly
4 garlic cloves, finely chopped
1 apple, cored and cubed in 1-inch pieces
¾ cup cider vinegar
¼ cup water (more if needed)
½ cup brown sugar
½ cup raisins
1 teaspoon salt
1 tablespoon finely chopped ginger
1 tablespoon yellow mustard seeds
2 star anise
1 large jalapeno, stemmed and seeded, chopped fine

1.   Literally every ingredient can go into the large saucepan, and when it comes to a boil, turn the mixture down to a simmer.

2.   You may need to add more hot water, but simmer until it is a jam consistency.

Note: My family especially likes this condiment served with duck, chicken, or turkey. Pork chops too.

Anita Ripple's Angel Food Cake

I grew up in the forties and fifties when mothers stayed home, wore aprons most of the day, and gossiped among one another in their free time. Anita Ripple and her family lived a few doors down the block, and she and my mother chatted a great deal about food while I played with the Ripple kids.

When I was about twelve years old, a happy event occurred when we were invited into Mrs. Ripple's kitchen for a slice of her fabulous Angel Food cake topped with pink "Seven Minute Frosting." I talked so much about that cake that my mother asked Mrs. Ripple for the recipe.

"You and your family come over for dinner Saturday night and I'll make the cake for dessert," was her response.

Boy, was I happy about that, but mother was not so happy because the Ripples had a bar in their living room and liked to drink. Unfortunately, so did my father and he often didn't know when to stop. The night of the dinner I thought everyone acted okay at the dinner table, and that was after drinks. All I could really remember was wondering when the Angel Food Cake was going to be served.

Mrs. Ripple finally got around to slicing us big pieces. She was acting kind of silly I thought, grinning a lot and giggling too, but the cake sure looked great. I dug into my piece and was about to say something about the crunchiness of the cake. I never remembered it with a crunch. My mother turned to me with a look that said, don't say a word. We all took small pieces of something out of our mouth after each bite of cake and set them on our plates. But Mrs. Ripple didn't, she just smiled and ate her angel food cake.

On our walk home, I said to my mother, "Why was the cake so crunchy?"

My Mother replied in a huff, "Anita Ripple likes to drink when she bakes, and she threw in the eggshells with the whites."

Angel Food Cake

In my teens, my girlfriends and I thought this was the epitome of a sophisticated dessert, and angel food cakes were beginning to be sold in bakeries.

Ingredients

1 angel food cake sliced into generous sized pieces

½ pint of whipping cream (not from a can), whipped

6 ounces of peanut brittle ground fine (reserve a few large pieces for garnish)

1.   In a processor or a blender process the peanut brittle to a rough crumble.

2.   Fold the peanut brittle into the whipped cream, leaving streaks of the brittle.

3.   Top each slice of cake with a dollop of whipping cream and garnish with larger pieces of brittle.

My First Delicatessen and My Second

Growing up in Los Angeles and not far from the Fairfax district, as soon as my friends and I could legally drive, we went to the delicatessens that served great sandwiches, fabulous salads, and delicious bakery goods. These deli-bakeries were all considered Jewish, and best of all they were open late into the evening. There were no fast-food hangouts in the fifties, so we congregated at these delis on weekends or after a late movie. We loved the banter of the waitresses, who seemed as old as God to us. And there was always the exciting possibility of spotting the occasional movie star out late enjoying the same fare.

A decade later, I traveled to Mexico City to visit a very different kind of delicatessen where the food was also good, but the customers and staff could not be more different.

The "Bellinghausen" was located in the "zona rosa," a tony tourist district in the Districo Federal and heart of the city. It was a safe and attractive area to stroll among posh shops that enjoyed a flourishing commerce. Prominently placed in the midst of this affluent area was a German delicatessen. The floor was laid with small white octagonal tiles. It amplified the chatter of the restaurant sounds almost loud enough to drown out the umpa music. The interior was decorated with steins, hand crafts, and photos of Germany. The waiters were all male, wore long white aprons, were most efficient, and humorless.

The diners were mostly men ranging from thirty-to-fifty years in age. Many were minus a limb; some wore black eye patches and several used canes. The evidence of severe burns hideously scarred an occasional face. leaving a man with a ghoulish look. Their clothing was impeccable: creased trousers and pressed jackets, but suspiciously made from military dress uniforms, minus insignias, patches, and medals.

I don't remember any women. The men spoke German exclusively and knotted themselves into boisterous groups where they toasted one another with private steins, ate pork sausages, potatoes, cabbage, and black bread with gluttony. When many of them got up to leave, it was with the aid of crutches, a chair, or a comrade's shoulder, and their exits were punctuated with flourishing salutes and clicking heels.

They owned the place and knew it, whether they had a financial stake in the restaurant or not. Even though they lost the war, their hubris was intact. Tourists would sometimes stare at them, and they would return the look with belligerent arrogance.

As history has proven, many Germans settled in Mexico City and ultimately developed a school of engineering, showing the Mexican construction industry how to safely build high-rise structures on the marsh lands of the Pre-Columbian Aztec city, Tenochtitlan. In the decades that followed, Mercedes and Volkswagen plants followed.

The Bellingshausen was the enclave of Nazi officers who somehow were able to escape capture, probably with money and influence. Here they would gather, drink, and eat foods they couldn't resist, like sauerbraten, pickled beets, and potato pancakes with applesauce.

Steamed Spiced Sauerkraut

An elderly French woman, married to a German, once gave me this recipe.

Ingredients

1 large can of sauerkraut, drained and washed

1 large onion, halved and sliced thin

1 pound of bacon cut into ½ inch pieces

salt to taste plus 2 cups of water

2 large Russet potatoes, peeled and quartered

5 juniper berries

6 pepper corns

2 bay leaves

¼ teaspoon caraway seeds

1 whole allspice

1.	Sauté the onions with the bacon until nearly cooked then add sauerkraut, water, and potatoes. You will want the bacon about half cooked.

2.   When the pot is simmering, add the balance of ingredients tied in a cheesecloth.

3.   Cook until the potatoes are done. Add salt to taste.

Irena

When I lived in Mexico City, many years past, I was most fortunate to have Irena as our creada (maid), as domestic workers were then referred. My husband and I lived in a two-story building where we occupied a comfortable apartment on the second floor. For a modest fee, many of the apartment dwellers, mostly Americans, used Irena for daily house cleaning and laundry arrangements. It was some time before I realized she lived on the roof of the apartment building with her handicapped son.

"The roof!" I said.

"Si, Señora, el techo," (roof), Irena replied.

Some roofs, actually many of them, have walls that extend around the perimeter. This creates a kind of roofless room, and those who must live there create a makeshift dwelling with various mats for the floor and fabric coverings to keep out the weather. Also, on many roofs, sinks of coarse lava stone are built-in where laundry is done.

When I learned of her humble living arrangements, and the son she raised as a single mother, I would always see that she had extra food for her and her boy. Her son couldn't have been more than six to eight years old, and it appeared he was a slow learner. She believed it was too dangerous to leave him on the roof alone, and rightly so. And that is why by day, when he was in school, she came downstairs to work.

She approached me one day to ask a favor that embarrassed her greatly. Her son's birthday was around the corner, and she wondered if I could make him a cake. She assured me that she would work extra hours and she would pay for the ingredients.

I have always been a good cook but one who avoids baking desserts, not to mention that Mexico is seven to eight thousand feet high and the baking rules I grew up with at sea level didn't apply here. Lucky me, that I had The Joy of Cooking cookbook that has the formula for high altitude baking. Still, as much as I wanted to say yes to Irena, I didn't want to risk making a full-sized cake and it being a failure. I explained to her that I would make her cupcakes, with absolutely no charge, nor would I expect extra labor on her part. She wept and said that small cakes would be even better for her son's friends—they could all have their own cakes. I put white frosting on the little cakes, because no food coloring was available to me in the local markets then. I boiled a beet and reduced the liquid then dotted the white frosting with the juice. I swirled the tops with a toothpick to give a rainbow effect. She thought I was a magician and had tears in her eyes as she carried them to the roof where her son's friends waited. The cupcakes were a hit.

The next day she insisted she do something for me. It didn't take me long to suggest that she show me how to make mole. The next day she arrived with all the ingredients, cooked with me, and in great detail explained exactly how to make a gorgeous pot of the dark rich mixture with cubes of pork swimming through it. Before she left that day, I slipped several pesos into her apron pocket without her knowledge.

To this day, I reproduce her mole during New Years.

Pork Loin Circles with Quick Green Mole

This recipe is dramatically shortened and very different from the native original. It also uses just one chili. *You can grill the tomatillos and other vegetables alongside the pork. This is a favorite of my daughter-in-law, Diane.

Ingredients – The Pork

1 pork loin cut into ½ inch circles (a meat cutter will do this, but it is a simple process)

1 tablespoon olive oil

1 tablespoon dried coriander

salt and pepper

1.   Place the pork, olive oil and coriander in a plastic bag and massage it well to coat the pork well. Refrigerate for about 30 minutes.

2.   Grill the pork loin circles until they reach 155 to 160 degrees. Remove and salt and pepper them, then tent them with a piece of foil.

Ingredients – The Mole

6 tomatillos, husked, washed, and halved
4 cloves of garlic
1 white onion cut into quarters
1 jalapeno halved the long way
1 small bunch of cilantro
juice of 3 or 4 limes
2 tablespoons chunky style peanut butter

1.   Grill the tomatillos, garlic, onions, and jalapeno chile until they are charred. Then puree them in a blender with the cilantro, peanut butter, lime juice and a little water. Add sea salt to taste.

2.   Warm the sauce and slip the pork circles into the pan of sauce.

Note: A pork loin is very lean and about 2 or 3 inches in diameter. The loins often come prepackaged.

Second Note: Tomatillos are green and round with a paper-like outer covering, which is easily removed. They look like a green tomato but are related to the gooseberry.

*If your grill is large enough, you can grill the pork and vegetables at the same time. Just pay attention to the doneness of the pork as it will toughen if over cooked.

Dinner at the Tropicana

We arrived in fancy (then called cocktail dresses), wearing our gemmy cocktail rings ready to order a boozy cocktail. Our husbands were attired in three-piece suits, studded tacks on their silk ties. We looked forward to dining at the most prestigious dinner house on the strip, the Tropicana. This was very early in Las Vegas. A maître d' greeted us with pomp and reviewed our reservation as though it was a resume. He then turned our party of four over to a friendlier Captain, a man in charge of the male waiters. Then, there wasn't a woman to be found in the dining room, and certainly not the kitchen. We followed the Captain across plush, garish carpeting, passing flocked papered walls and observed ourselves in strategically placed mirrors. After seating us in a huge leather-tufted booth, our waiter engaged in some small talk, querying us about our geography and food likes. Honestly, there was little to know about the foods we favored. We were all in our late twenties, from L.A., not yet traveled, and hungry for a grand elegant food experience. We were sure the classic items on this Continental menu would give us that. We were full of ourselves and felt fortunate that we could afford the exorbitant prices listed on the menu.

Our stiff waiter surprised us by standing like a soldier and addressing us with a German accent. He could have easily exchanged his tuxedo for a military uniform and been cast in a Hollywood war movie. Then, accents were an added attraction in expensive restaurants. He expounded on the preparations of lobster, pheasant, and sturgeon. With elaborate description, he labored over the chef's ability to prepare lamb and beef items as well.

After ending his long descriptions, we were all relieved but confused as to what to order due to the many choices he had presented. We were all quiet. My husband broke the silence with, "I'll have a cheeseburger and she'll have a chili dog."

My Cheeseburger Rules

1.   Always toast the bun and preferably a sesame seed bun

2.   Mix your own secret sauce (a mix of mayo catsup, sweet mustard, etc.)

3.   Use a ¼ pound of ground beef, not too lean

4.   A slice of American cheese melts best and is creamy

5.   A slice of raw, purple onion

6.   A thick slice of beefsteak tomato

7.   A large piece of iceberg lettuce (for crunch)

Note: In the past I never used American cheese, but most chefs prefer it for melting. I agree. Other cheeses take over the taste of the burger, like Swiss and cheddar. American cheese melts well as it is made with additional milk products.

Christmas Dinner

When I married and had my own family, at some point I took over the cooking of Christmas dinner, as daughters often do. My Anglo mother had always made a pork roast with pink applesauce that she colored with red-hot candies until I explained that the skins from Rome apples would give her the same color and a stick of cinnamon would give her the flavor. She also made scalloped potatoes, creamed spinach, which I'm sorry to say, included Campbell's Cream of Mushroom soup, and we always started with coleslaw. It was a good and satisfying dinner. But I had an ethnic side; my father was both Spanish and Indian and came from a food culture I had been exposed to early in life. Being an adventurous cook besides, I wanted to try something new for Christmas.

My mother liked to tell the story of leaving her Anglo family's home to marry my father. She told her parsimonious mother the day she left, "And when I peel my potatoes, I'll peel the skins off this thick," using her thumb and forefinger as a quarter inch guide. Mother liked being dramatic as much as her mother preferred being reserved. That very WASPish side of the family loathed the day my mother married a man of color, but that's another story. Mother completely embraced the cooking of Mexican food. She even accomplished making excellent flour tortillas, and good salsa that pleased my father immeasurably. She spoke Spanish fluently and became a good translator.

So, following her lead, my plan for Christmas was to make tamales from scratch and a mole sauce. This was no easy task as it was before Mexican food items were available in ethnic stores, not to mention supermarkets. There was the masa to make with lard, the cornhusks, and proper chilies to find and process. A pot of simmering pork shoulder, with spices, needed to be on a burner most of the day to ensure delicious and tender meat. The broth was needed for the tamales and the mole, a sauce comprised of everything from chilies to chocolate to a ripe banana. I had lived for a time in Mexico City a few years earlier, and fortunately had an authentic mole recipe. After rummaging through several Mexican markets, I found all my esoteric ingredients. I knew how it would please my dad, for me to make this very authentic dish.

When my father entered my house on Christmas Eve, it pleased me when he said, "It smells like tamales!" We sat at my beautiful new dining table that I had set with colorful Mexican touches. Proudly I produced warm tamales right out of the steamer, and before we unfolded them from their husks my mother covered her face with her hands, cried dramatically and said, "I want to go home!" My father and I looked blankly at one another. I had no idea that changing the traditional menu would have such a negative effect on my mother.

I learned that day that we all have our ethnic roots, and at the end of my Christmas dinner I had to assure Mother that in the future we would return to her traditional, Anglo Christmas dinner. Now we have tamales on New Year's Eve.

Masa for Tamales

Today I highly recommend you buy prepared masa from your local Mexican deli.

Ingredients

½ pound lard
12 cups of dry masa
8 cups water
3 tablespoons salt

1.   Beat all the above ingredients with a standing electric mixer until you have a very smooth masa. Cooks often add a little of the meat broth in the masa. When I make tamales, I fill them with mole (recipes on pages 32 and 139).

Napkins

When my oldest daughter, Diana, was about five years old, she wanted to be included in a sit-down dinner party I had planned for out-of-town guests. I said that if she would use her napkin and her place setting like a grown-up, she would be welcomed. She thought this was no problem and was somewhat indignant that I would even bring up her table manners.

Once we were all seated, a party of about twelve as I remember, we proceeded with a formal dinner. Diana was polite, and used the proper spoon for her cauliflower soup, and knife and fork well for her roast chicken and potatoes, but somehow had forgotten to put her napkin on her lap. I waited to see if she would remember but she didn't. She was sitting closer to her father than me, so I quietly called to her, not using her name, "Put your napkin on your lap."

An adult man seated next to me turned bright red, picked up his napkin and snapped it onto his lap.

Cream of Cauliflower Soup

This is such an easy soup to make and is always received well.

Ingredients

2 tablespoons olive oil

2 tablespoons butter

1 medium sized head of cauliflower broken into florets

1 small onion, coarsely chopped

4 cups of chicken broth

½ cup whipping cream

salt and pepper

grated nutmeg for garnish

1.   Sauté cauliflower and onion in olive oil and butter using a four-quart pan. When ingredients are hot and sticky, add chicken broth.

2.   Cover and simmer for 15 minutes then blend with an immersion blender. Salt and pepper to tase.

3.   Garnish with nutmeg.

Note: The nutmeg is important.

Thanksgiving Gravy

A few days after Thanksgiving, when the turkey tastes best and the gravy even better, I walked a large and crowded tray of our turkey leftovers to a coffee table in the living room. I was particularly proud of my gravy as I had just learned to use Madeira Portuguese wine to enhance the sauce, and I couldn't believe how greatly the liquor improved the gravy's flavor. The leftovers would be a hearty lunch and liberate the refrigerator. Everyone was oohing and aahing when they saw our turkey leftovers, and that was about the time I tripped. Surprisingly, I was able to salvage most of the food on the tray–but not the gravy.

The delicious brown sauce landed all over the base of a wrought iron table, a base that was festooned with hammered leaves and roses. How was I ever going to get it clean? I was so annoyed with myself. I stood wondering what to do next, when I looked out the large glass sliding door and there was my answer. It was Max, our one hundred and-eighty-pound Mastiff. He looked back at me from the yard with an expression that said, "Can I help?"

Max rushed into the living room and went straight for the wrought iron base lathered in gravy. For this task, he got very serious and used a combat crawl to wedge himself as close as he could to the gravy-soaked area under the table. He stayed there, licking at the wrought iron leaves and roses and surrounding area for at least an hour. From then on whenever Max was invited into the house, the wrought iron table would always get a few licks.

Easy Turkey Pan Gravy with Madeira

Eliminate excess grease from the roasting pan (where you will make gravy) by placing a paper towel on top, and then remove it for disposal. This works like magic. If you have roasted your turkey with carrots, onions, celery, and a bouquet garni, you can leave them in the pan while you make gravy.

Ingredients

1 degreased turkey pan

¼ cup of Madeira

6 tablespoons softened butter and 6 tablespoons flour combined

6 cups chicken or turkey stock

salt to taste

1.   Put the roasting pan on one or two burners and when hot deglaze with Madeira.

2.	After alcohol burns off, add stock, and bring back to simmer.

3.	Begin adding flour/butter mixture using a whisk until you get desired thickness and salt to taste

Note: The French taught us this simple technique and it avoids the roux making process. If you want a thicker gravy, add more flour mixture; if you want a thinner gravy add more broth.

Second Note: Just remember to cook out the flour taste for a few minutes. You can remove the vegetables and bouquet garni but no need to strain the gravy.

Hot Spaghetti / Cold Spaghetti

Over the weekend heavy winds off the sea had blown our yard apart, and the grandparents were there to help. We stayed outside working well past lunch, and we were all cold and hungry when we came inside, especially the children. I made a hearty lunch for my in-laws and our family.

I scurried to get the kids fed first and then announced that the adults' lunch was ready. The pot of spaghetti was good and hot when I plated the food.

My husband charged into his bowl of pasta like a mad dog. His first bite came flying out of his mouth, followed by a long-winded growl about how food should never be served at a molten temperature, and what the hell was I trying to do . . . set his mouth on fire? My mother returned to the kitchen with his bowl of spaghetti and a look of wonderment.

I grabbed the plate, emptied it into a steel bowl, threw open the freezer door, grabbed a handful of ice cubes and tossed the spaghetti with the ice like I was tossing a salad. Mother looked on in more wonderment.

My husband ate his watered-down, but not molten spaghetti with delight and then spent the rest of the day apologizing to me for his harsh words.

My Vodka Pasta

This is not the pasta in my story, but my favorite one to date. A pot of boiling water with angel hair pasta should be on the stove while making this recipe so you may use the starchy water to thicken the pasta sauce. It is a good idea to cook the pasta ahead and reserve one to two cups of the starch water.

Ingredients

2 tablespoons olive oil
2 tablespoons butter
2 shallots minced
¼ cup vodka
2 to 3 tablespoons tomato paste
1 cup of pasta water, or more
¼ cup whipping cream
½ cup Parmesan cheese finely grated
parsley finely chopped
1 pound of angel hair pasta cooked

salt and pepper

1.   Sauté shallots in olive oil and butter.

2.   Add tomato paste and when mixed into the butter and shallots, add the vodka. Ladle pasta water into the skillet until you have a sauce. Cook for a few minutes

3.   Add cream and when your sauce is hot, add al dente pasta and most of the Parmesan cheese. Salt and pepper to taste. Garnish with parsley.

Note: I have read that this pasta arrived in Italy in the eighties where the sauce contained sausage and crushed tomatoes. It arrived in the U.S. this way.

Ants

I decided that we had built our house on an anthill, so aggressive was the invasion of the insects into our home. They were in the bathroom looking for water, the kitchen looking for food, the garage we didn't know what for, and they forever marched the perimeter of the house. It was one of the first words in Spanish (ormigas) our daughter, Juliet, learned.

When my daughter was three, she cried when we killed the insets, so we did a lot of that when she wasn't looking. They were into our food and water daily. I hated the idea of using poison, but the ants had become so invasive that we were beginning to think of that alternative but decided against it. I figured that you had to be smarter than an ant to outwit them, so I went to the library to learn if there was a safer solution. All I learned was that they had a unique society based on survival. For instance, scouts were sent to look for food and water and return home with their intelligence. When the tribe followed the scout's directive and the food was not there, they would kill him. I didn't return to the library for more research after learning that!

One night we hosted a charity event, and Juliet stayed up well past her three-year-old bedtime and became very difficult when I tried putting her to bed. She was exhausted but knew she hadn't yet had dessert, and that this was a party night, and that meant dessert was somewhere in the house. Determined she was not going to bed without, she spied a cake with white icing and chocolate sprinkles. She looked at me as if to say, "you see I found it and I want it, cut me a slice."

I walked over to the cake, and with a critical eye examined it. I turned to her shaking my head and said, "Ormigas." She said with a whimper and a wrinkled chin, "Ormigas," and ever so reluctantly let me put her to bed. I had fooled her into thinking that the sprinkles were ormigas, not chocolate sprinkles.

Cake and Ganache

You'll learn from these recipes that I make as few desserts as possible, and as simply as possible.

Ingredients

Pound cake sliced
8 ounces of bittersweet chocolate
1 cup heavy whipping cream
2 teaspoons vanilla
2 to 3 tablespoons rum (optional)
Vanilla ice cream and ganache

1. Place bittersweet chocolate, whipping cream, and vanilla in a glass measuring cup and microwave for a minute or two until chocolate is melted. Remove from the microwave and whip until glossy.

2.   Place a scoop of vanilla ice cream on top of each slice of cake and top with ganache.

Russian Coffee

It was time to entertain the employees of the three health spas our family owned. The businesses were doing well, the staff were all hard working, and we had just settled in our new home, which was a great party house. About twenty guests had arrived. I knew most of them, but not everyone's date.

The party took place in the eighties when hair was big. It was teased, almost always blonde, and worn up or down, but inevitably big. It seemed to me the largest dos were on the dumbest heads. That night I was proven right.

A buxom blonde, as they used to call them in the days of Monroe and Mansfield, sauntered into our living room on the arm of one of our managers. She brandished an astonishing head of extreme hair, and paraded about in gold stiletto heels, a low-cut red dress sporting the posture of a Marine drill sergeant. Did I mention her dress was red, tight, and very short?

I had grown used to some of the people that were attracted to health spas, especially during this decade. They could be incredibly absorbed with their physical image. She (we'll call her Marilyn) was one of those types. Her hair never moved the entire evening, but her body never stopped undulating, and she navigated toward my husband. In fact, all evening, she was never more than an arm's length from him.

After I served my lovely buffet, Marilyn seemed to gain steam, and was now patting my husband on his chest as she spoke to him. And he, like the dumb man he had temporarily become, was flattered. I heard her voice become low, and her fat lips slowly say, "Would you please show me the rest of your lovely big house?" That entire night I practiced self-control, and found a way not to speak to Marilyn, so as not to slash and destroy her with my tongue.

Before the evening's end, I served small cups of Russian coffee as a dessert. It was a popular drink then; a mixture of hot chocolate and espresso coffee that everybody enjoyed. Marilyn had become quite arrogant around me by the end of the evening, or jealous, however you wanted to read her. As I offered her a cup, she said,

"Ew, what is that?"

I replied in the low voice of a Satanic witch, "Drink it or I will pour it on your hair."

My husband's business partner was the only one who heard me. He laughed so uproariously he went over backwards in his chair.

Russian Coffee Recipe

Russian coffee was a fad when coffee houses were common in the '60s, and the drink eventually entered mainstream cooking.

Ingredients

6 tablespoons instant espresso
6 tablespoons cocoa powder
6 teaspoons of sugar
4 cups evaporated milk
2 cups water
pinch of cinnamon for garnish
pinch of salt

1.   Place all the ingredients in a saucepan over moderate heat and whisk until it simmers.

2.   Adjust the taste for sweetness, and a pinch of salt brings out flavor in the drink.

Note: You can vary the quantities of the ingredients according to your taste.

A Christmas Cocktail Party

It was Christmas, and we were invited to a neighborhood cocktail party. I had hosted parties like this and learned that American guests ate heartily from the hors d'oeuvres table. I say Americans because in Mexico City, where I had lived for two years, guests seemed to pick lightly at such faire, and go on to a late dinner. I found the same in France. Here, however, I learned these parties sufficed as dinner and cookbooks suggested to prepare twenty bites per person! The hostess asked if I wouldn't mind bringing my well-known guacamole, a recipe I brought back with me from living in Mexico City. I didn't think guacamole was appropriate for a cocktail party, but I was a food snob then.

71

The day had been a busy one, and I didn't calculate how long it would take me to get ready. My silky dress, my shiny pink stockings, that necessitated my sixties garter belt, and then there was the beehive hairdo. This look was far from slipping into a jogging suit. After stepping into my very high heels, I took a deep breath and headed for the refrigerator when I heard my husband call, "Let's walk, it's only a block."

"Okay," I returned, "but you carry the guacamole."

We started down the street, and I squealed, "I forgot my ring!" He stood, looking annoyed like men can in such moments. I couldn't miss showing off my new princess ring, stacked like a mini-pyramid. And after all it was a cocktail ring. We arrived a bit late, but I got the guacamole unwrapped and placed on the table, then was promptly handed a gin gimlet, which I downed like a glass of water. Another soon followed when I decided to sit down. A third gimlet arrived which I tried to sip when I realized I was terribly thirsty. Water was nowhere, so I headed for the kitchen wobbling a bit, I noticed. Along the way, I kept hearing how great my guacamole was and how I must send out the recipe. It was always that way when I showed up with the famous dip and chips. I couldn't exactly explain why, but the compliments began to annoy me–could it be the gimlets? I decided I should eat and stop drinking. Hmmm. I remembered my dip was good and stood with guests dipping into the green sauce. I felt quite superior when we got home that evening after all the compliments I had received, until I looked down at my ring.

It was napped in guacamole.

Stone-Age Guacamole

Having lived in Mexico City for some time, I learned to make what I think is the best guacamole ever. You'll find no limes in this recipe, as it was shipping that brought citrus to the new world, so this is likely a pre-Columbian guacamole.

Ingredients

½ medium white onion, coarsely chopped

1 medium jalapeno chile seeded, stems removed and coarsely chopped

1/2 cup cilantro leaves, coarsely chopped

¼ teaspoon salt

1 or 2 tablespoons water

2 avocados, lightly mashed

avocado seeds

½ cup chopped tomatoes

1.   Puree the onion, chile and salt, cilantro and water using a small processor.

2.   Add the puree to the lightly mashed avocado and incorporate well.

3.   Lightly fold in the tomatoes. Correct the salt for taste then garnish with the avocado seed.

Note: Making a puree of the onion, chile, salt and cilantro is duplicating the pestle and mortar method used in the Stone-Age period. This is the key to making this green fruit into a memorable savory recipe.

A Special Salad

My husband came into the kitchen about noon one Sunday and said, "Can you make a quick lunch for four? Some guys are coming over for a business meeting."

Well, I could, but I would have preferred to go to the market. I said yes and flew into my dressing room to change from my robe, put on a dash of eye make-up and a bit of lotion. Now I was ready to find something for lunch.

As I pulled open the lower drawer of the refrigerator, I thought it would have to be a big salad. A little of this green, a little of that, and I could open a can of garbanzo beans and maybe some pimentos. Guys liked those tastes. I could garnish it with that last avocado that had become ripe, maybe some sunflower seeds. Yes, a lunch salad was coming together.

I had everything in the bowl and had poured a hearty dressing over the salad when my husband came into the kitchen and asked if I could serve them NOW. They all wanted to leave and visit a building site that was the topic of their meeting.

In my haste, I tossed the salad with my clean hands, not the salad tongs. Lunch was wolfed down, and they were gone. But one guy on his way out, said, "That was a very different salad."

I said, "I hope that means it was good."

He said, "Yeah, it was good, but really different. I am trying to figure out the spice in the dressing."

Then it dawned on me. The spice in the dressing was the lemon scented hand lotion I had put on earlier.

My Special Salad Recipe

Clearly, I can no longer duplicate that salad dressing as I no longer use that hand lotion!

Ingredients

1 head of romaine lettuce, chopped fine

½ cup chopped celery

1 medium cucumber, halved and sliced

1 can garbanzo beans, drained

1 avocado, cubed

½ cup sliced pimentos

½ cup black olives

1.   Toss with the dressing:

        ¼ cup olive oil

        ¼ cup sherry vinegar

        ¼ cup sunflower seeds

        salt and pepper to taste

2.   Blend the ingredients in a blender. If the dressing thickens too much, add a little water.

Persimmons

As my in-laws grew all manner of vegetables and fruits on their property, I was pleased to be able to introduce this produce to my kids early in their lives. They got to taste and see vegetables pulled from the soil of their grandparent's gardens, as well as climb fruit trees to sample ripe fruits. Apricots, plumbs, and peaches were favorites. I remember the work it was for me to deal with the large quantities of ripe fruits. Unless I got busy, a kitchen of swarming gnats soon invaded my kitchen, and since I was not a canner, I had to get creative. I enjoyed cooking but not the process of preserving foods in jars.

I thought I was clever when the peach crop would get out of hand. After giving them a rough chop, I would add them to equal parts of soft vanilla ice cream, then refreeze my mixture. It was an understatement to call that dessert a hit, and a real treat in the winter to taste fresh peaches, again.

One day in the fall my daughter, who was about six years old, watched me slice in half a soft persimmon (at the equator) that came from her grandparents' trees. I showed her how to eat it with a spoon. She seemed fascinated by the color and texture, and with gusto took her first bite.

Her response was "I can't eat this! It's full of strings and hairs."

Hayashi Persimmons Tips

1.   These are soft persimmons and very sweet. They are delicious scooped from their center and served with ricotta cheese.

2.   Hayashis when pureed (with their skins) are also delicious incorporated into melted vanilla ice cream and frozen.

3.   Also, you can put them into the freezer for about 15 minutes then slice circles of the fruit and serve with cheese and quarters of cut limes as a dessert.

Chinese Menu

My husband and I had a favorite Chinese restaurant that we frequented, but we had a problem with the menu. It was far too large, a collection of page after page of complicated dishes that you ordered by the number. You could have changed clothes behind this menu. We stayed with the same old order because it was delicious, and because we didn't want to venture further into the restaurant's huge number of choices, none of which we understood.

One night, I decided we should be adventurous and suggested we take some time to really scrutinize the dishes. We did but we were stilled baffled about what to select. The Chinese waiter was growing impatient when we still hadn't decided. We had tried to ask his help, but for our ears his broken English defied the food descriptions.

There he stood pencil in hand waiting to take our order. I said, picking numbers at random, "We'll take number 32, ah, number 48 and number 61." He dropped his hands to his sides, looked at us and said, "Boy, you guys really know how to order."

Potstickers

Some years ago, friends brought me potstickers from a restaurant. They were raving about them and asked if I could duplicate the recipe. I did.

The story goes: a chef let his wontons simmer so long they were stuck to the bottom of the pot, and to his credit he served them and called them potstickers.

Ingredients

oil for sautéing

1 package wonton skins (use the small ones unless you are adventurous)

1 tablespoon ginger, peeled and roughly chopped

4 cloves garlic

1 small jalapeno, stemmed and seeded

¼ pound ground pork and ¼ pound shrimp combined

2 green onions, chopped fine

2 tablespoons soy sauce

1 teaspoon sesame seed oil for garnish

1.   Turn on the processor using the steel blade and drop the ginger garlic and jalapeno down the feeding tube (this lessens the mincing time by half and does a better job).

2.   Take the top of the processor off and place the pork, shrimp, green onions, and soy sauce into the bowl and process until ingredients are like a fine meatloaf mixture.

3.   Place a teaspoon of the mixture in a wanton using a little water to seal.

4.   Sauté pot stickers in a skillet with a modest amount of oil until brown. Drizzle a small amount of water into the pan then cover and they will steam until done (just a few minutes).

Note: I like sweet soy sauce for dipping.

Eat Like a Horse

In the sixties, my husband was vice president of operations for the largest health club chain in the U.S. At that time, the CEO asked him to travel to Tokyo and learn if expansion into Japan was a good idea.

That plan ultimately found me in the heart of Tokyo and at a long dinner table of about twenty diners, all men. Bankers, we learned, owned the land in Tokyo, and they were entertaining us in an imperial fashion to gain insight into health clubs as well as to lease their land. My husband and I each had a personal interpreter. The restaurant saw that our food arrived, course after course, at a fast clip. I knew that, before many Americans had learned much about Japanese culture, I was getting an ear, eye, and mouth full.

One interpreter sat next to me at my end of the table while another sat with my husband at the opposite end. Looking back, I think we were being subtly and separately grilled about business during the noisy meal.

When the Japanese ate their various dishes, they held their bowls up to, and just below, their lower lip and then loudly slurped their soup or sauce, followed by shoveling the solid pieces into their mouths with the aid of chopsticks. It was a slurping and splashing kind of eating and I joined in to enjoy my food their way. I don't think I knew what fine and delicate foods I was eating though, or rather, slurping. But it was the noisiest dinner I have attended since.

My interpreter asked me a multitude of questions and seemed pleased I answered them all with alacrity. I think he saved the big question for last. "Does it really work when you do these exercises? Can you lose your fat this way?"

I answered by saying, "Yes, it does, but if you eat like a horse, you have to exercise like one." With a hand, he covered his broad smile and noisy giggle. Then he hit the bowl before him with his chopsticks until the guests stopped slurping and became still. He translated my comment to the diners, at which time they all convulsed with laughter so loudly, it brought the restaurant staff running.

Sukiyaki

When I returned from my visit to Japan, I could find little about their cooking, but I always enjoyed eating Sukiyaki at the few local Japanese restaurants that existed. So, I watched a few Japanese cooks prepare the dish at our table and devised my own recipe. It may not be as fashionable as it once was, but a very tasty and satisfying dish, and healthy too.

Ingredients

vegetable oil

1 pound tender steak sliced thin (place in freezer for half an hour for easy slicing).

6 green onions sliced 2 to 3 inches

small can bamboo shoots, drained

½ pound mushrooms, sliced

handful of bean sprouts

4 ribs Chinese cabbage sliced in 2-inch pieces

soy sauce to taste

sugar to taste

a splash of sake

1 package cellophane noodles

1. Use a wok or cast-iron skillet that is well oiled and hot. Begin by adding the strips of meat, quickly stirring them until the meat is no longer pink.

2. Then add in order the list of ingredients, being sure the mixture is hot before adding the next ingredient.

3. Adding sake and sugar at the end makes the dish Japanese.

Flying Geese

While driving, I said, "Look into the Mobile guide for a nice restaurant. Let's splurge tonight." It was the eighties, and my husband and I were on a road trip, and he was dozing in the passenger seat, not wanting to think about dining anywhere. I persisted.

"Okay, okay," he finally said. And sure enough, there was a five-star hotel and restaurant in North Carolina that we were driving through.

"I swear, you have special radar when it comes to sensing where good restaurants are," he said.

I did, and drove straight to this special Southern hotel, The Tides Inn. It was built much like a plantation, and we decided to stay the night. A blackboard in the hotel lobby greeted us with postings of the most recent guests. It read something like Mr. and Mrs. James Wentworth, Junior, and their daughters Melissa and Mercedes; Mr. and Mrs. Rupert Sheffield, III, and their son Jonathan and daughter Millicent, etc. We were from California and felt like hicks.

Relaxing in our rooms, we laughed about the snobbery of the modern South still wanting to emulate the past. We dressed well for dinner, or so we thought. It was summer and I wore a backless floral pantsuit with a shawl, which every woman scowled at who passed me. The scowlers wore dark-colored skirts, practical blouses, and tailored linen blazers. The men wore similar outfits. Both genders were big on crests emblazoned on the breast pockets of their jackets.

As we entered the dining room my husband was stopped in his tracks. An employee superciliously explained that an open collar was not the dress code in their dining room, and he would have to buy a tie in the hotel shop.

My husband suggested I be seated, and he would join me after buying a tie. I thought his tan suit, with a vest and modest floral shirt was good looking, but evidently only in California, and not by the view of the staff at the Tides Inn.

My husband soon returned looking annoyed. He flipped up his new purchase. "How do you like the fu . . . geese, flying west on my tie?" he said as he sat down for dinner.

Roasted Goose

I roasted a goose one Christmas, and we all enjoyed the flavor. But expect a turkey to be far meatier. The roasting of the goose reminded me of the phrase, there was never such a goose. A Christmas Carol, Charles Dickens.

Ingredients

1 goose, 10 to 12 pounds
salt and pepper
2 pounds small potatoes, halved

1.   Rub goose generously with salt and pepper and rest uncovered overnight in the refrigerator.

2.   Allow the goose to come to room temperature before roasting. Prick the goose well so fat can run off during roasting.

3.   Roast on a rack at 325 degrees for about an hour, then remove the accumulated goose fat (which you may want to retain) with a baster and roast for another hour.

4.   Add the potatoes around the goose and reduce the oven to 275 degrees, then roast another hour until done. Use your instant read thermometer and remove bird from the oven when breast temperature reads 155 degrees.

Note: It is important to keep the level of the fat low in the pan so as not to cause a fat fire. Rest the goose 20 to 30 minutes before carving, as it will allow carry over cooking and retain the bird's juices. Retained goose fat can be used like duck fat.

A Special Pâté

It was the early seventies, and my husband and I were in Paris eating in a cafe with no Americans in sight. We were at a classic bistro with noisy diners. A huge bouquet of fresh flowers languished on the corner of the brass-trimmed bar, like a beautifully-coiffed woman. We were drinking wonderful wine that was cheaply priced and enjoying the mood and setting.

Why had Americans developed just the "diner" or "burger joint" and not this comfortable neighborhood bistro where dinners were served hearty regional faire?

The room was packed with customers, the scent of the flowers came from behind me, and the look of the dishes coming out of the kitchen were enticing. Agile waiters walking at a near run, in long white aprons, deftly managed heavy trays hefted on their shoulders. The ceramic floor tiles amplified the loud sounds of the restaurant's commerce. We were seated at a small round table covered with white butcher paper. A ramekin filled with a pâté, and a long warm baguette were placed before us. "My God, taste the bread," I kept saying.

My husband said, "I think you'll like this stuff," pointing to the ramekin as he lathered a second knife-full out of the small container onto his bread.

I didn't like the pâté, I adored it, and had to know whose liver I was eating. With hand motions, we ordered another ramekin because Americans like to gorge on what they adore. The waiter rolled his eyes as he produced another. I tried to learn more, asking our waiter about the pâté, fumbling though my urban dictionary French terms while getting nowhere. I turned to another waiter who ignored me as if we were sullying the bistro. I walked to the bar with my inquiry, where the bartender looked at me with distaste, and basically told me to return to my table and sit down. These French knew how to handle pushy Americans.

My husband said, "This may be one time that you are not going to find out what you're eating."

But I was going to find out what I was eating. I wanted to reproduce it when I got home. I turned to a fellow diner and said, in pigeon-French, "What pâté are we eating?" He raised his shoulders then dropped them. In a mirror, I could see the bartender scoffing at me. Then a rather polite French gentleman tapped me on my shoulder and said, "American lady, let me zee zee book."

I handed him my dictionary, and he squinted at a word and said, "Et iss zat one." I anxiously took the book to read the word in English. In the interim my husband had ordered a third ramekin.

I stopped eating after reading the word and pushed the pâté away. I shook my head. "What's wrong, are we eating animal dung, or something?" My husband asked.

"No," I replied, "We have been eating pâté made from lark's livers . . ."

My Faux Pâté

I once made a pâté and didn't care much for it, but then I didn't grow up with that taste, or the knowledge how to make it properly. I have since made a faux mixture to spread on toast points at parties.

Ingredients

1 pound of Braunschweiger (smoked liverwurst)
6 hard-boiled eggs
½ cup parsley, chopped fine
6 cornichon pickles, chopped fine
mayonnaise to blend
white bread toast points
salt to taste

1.   Blend the above ingredients, but not in a food processor.

2.   Serve on toast.

Note: Calling this spread a pâté would make a French chef shudder, but it always draws good comments. Most Americans probably never grew up with pâté.

A Bridge to a Cake

When I still got along with my sister-in-law, I decided to bake her a birthday cake. I am no baker and seldom take on such a chore. She mentioned how she loved the flavor of lemon, so I set to my task. She was to arrive Sunday. I baked the cake Saturday, and it turned out well. Because we continually dealt with ants in the area where we lived, I worried about how to store the cake overnight. I was out of refrigerator room. I certainly didn't want them to attack the only cake I would make in probably a decade. Nothing resembled a cake holder in my kitchen. I had to set it somewhere overnight, so I devised my plan. I decided to fill a large skillet half with water, place a bowl upside down in the water, and the cake on top. I reckoned I had built a clever moat.

The next morning, George, my son of about thirteen, woke me. "Mother, Mother! You've got to see what the ants have done."

Oh no. I immediately conjured visions of my cake covered with ants. But how could that have happened. I charged into the kitchen to view an extraordinary event.

Throughout the night, ants had plunged into the water to drown themselves, and somehow connect to one another to build a bridge of dead comrades. The rest of the clan marched across the mortal bridge and were just about to reach my cake.

I decided it was an omen. I would never bake another cake. And I haven't.

Slices of Pound Cake with Lemon Custard

The food Lover's Companion describes Zabaglione as one of Italy's great gifts to the rest of the world. Zabaglione is an ethereal dessert made by whisking together egg yolks, wine (traditionally Marsala,) and sugar. I made this dessert sauce obsessively when I learned about it in Chef's school and used every liquor imaginable. When I used Limoncello, I found I had a lemon custard. An elderly Frenchman gave me his take on this recipe which is very old world.

Ingredients - Zabaglione

1 egg yolk

½ an eggshell filled with white sugar (not to the rim)

1 eggshell of Limoncello

1.   Whip the egg yolk and sugar in a bowl over simmering water until thick.

2.   Stir in the Limoncello well and you have a warm lemon custard.

Note: This was my first dessert in a fine Italian restaurant. It was made classically and poured into a flute. l knew little of classic food at the time, and said to the waiter, "This is warm." The seasoned waiter shook his head and looked at me with a look that an ignorant American will always remember.

Second Note: This recipe serves one or two, but easily doubles.

Diana's First Cafeteria Experience

One weekend morning the family was gathered around the kitchen table enjoying chat time after breakfast. I don't know why I asked the question of my six-year-old.

"So, Diana, did anything interesting happen at school this week?"

"Nope." It was her stock reply.

I sensed that something of interest had happened, as we mothers do, so I pursued the topic.

"How do you like eating in the cafeteria?"

This was a new experience for her, and as a family of foodies we often discussed food stories after a meal.

With an embarrassed grin, she covered her mouth, clearly holding back a unique event that happened in the cafeteria.

"Did something funny happen there, yesterday?" I persisted.

She nodded but didn't take her hand away from her mouth.

"Well tell us, we like a funny story."

She set her hand on the table, and with a crooked smile told her story.

"Well, we had hot dogs for lunch, and Roland took his out of the bun and sipped it into his pants. He walked around the cafeteria with it hanging out, and Mrs. Fox went c-r-a-z-y . . ."

Bratwurst on a Roll (Family Favorite Dog)

Ingredients

1 warmed bratwurst per roll - steamed or grilled
Kaiser
Coleslaw (DIY below)
deli mustard

Ingredients - Coleslaw

½ head of cabbage, roughly cut
1 carrot, roughly cut
2 green onions, roughly cut
1 to 2 tablespoons cider vinegar
1 teaspoon sugar
mayonnaise to blend
salt to taste

1.   Place all ingredients in the processor, minus the mayonnaise and pulse until the raw items are ground fine.

2.   Remove the ground items and add your desired amount of mayonnaise.

3.   Assemble your buns and bratwurst, coleslaw, and mustard on your Kaiser roll to make a great sandwich.

Food and Pleasure for Paradise

Our family had great friends who lived on a large ranch in the four corners area of the United States. Part of their vast acreage was located on a Pueblo III site (1100-1300 A.D.). We were allowed to dig there if we granted UCLA the pick of our finds. The items we found were not of intrinsic value; the terracotta pieces were crude, yet the stone implements like metates and manos (grinding stone and pestles) were well-hewn. Along with many handcrafted items, these people had a captivating lifestyle that I felt privileged to learn about.

We were digging in a room about twelve feet square with walls of neatly stacked stones; large stones that made the dwelling safe, a thickness of about a foot; when I found a burial that had been placed in the wall. Archeologists call this an intrusion burial, and it almost always applies to very young children whose spirit the family wishes to hold close. As I cleared off this wall area with a trowel, a stone came loose and there was my burial, about the size of a small watermelon. Out of it, I carefully removed a tiny skull, likely of a newborn. Next came the beak of a tropical parrot and his claws. Also in the infant's grave were tiny bowls that held minute remnants of corn cobs, and finally a small rattle. In paradise, the baby was to enjoy her food, be amused by her parrot and play with her rattle.

The heartfelt story of her funerary artifact also told the story of corn, and how it sustained the people of the Americas for thousands of years. All the items were buried with the child to enjoy in the next life, but the parrot had been sacrificed and traded up from a tropical area, maybe hundreds of miles away. It had likely been a coveted rarity in the household. When the family sacrificed the bird to join their baby, it must have been with the deepest love. The rattle was the size of a walnut shell and when you shook it, the sound of small rocks inside clattered.

Popcorn

Although I do not have a pre-Columbian recipe to share with you, I will mention that it was the Native American who gave us popcorn. Tiny corn cobs that we sometimes found in burials were the size of your thumb. Here is a quick recipe for popcorn.

Ingredients

Popping corn
Butter
Powdered jalapeno chilis

1.   Make popcorn according to instructions on package.

2.   In a separate saucepan, heat butter until liquid. Add a few pinches of jalapeno chili powder.

3.   Pour butter mixture onto popcorn and salt to taste.

Buying Food at the Chandlery

We were moored in Lisbon, with a crew of twenty-five and passengers of the same number. Yes, you read that right. It was a barefoot cruise in the eighties allowing everyone onboard to participate in the sailing of the ship. With ten-thousand square feet of sail, the old ship was one-hundred and sixty-five feet in length. The crew accepted the extra help, sometimes with aplomb, sometimes not.

We were about to sail to Antigua, in the West Indies of the Caribbean. It was estimated to take twenty-one days to landfall. Because I had a chef's background, I was appointed to purchase food stores for the fifty people on board. I was told to buy foodstuffs to feed fifty people, three times daily for twenty-one days. The captain told me this like he was asking for a bowl of soup. So clearly, I had to find the local chandlery, a warehouse of food and many other things. The crew was of mixed heritage, two Brits, a German, Netherlanders, and a Zulu. I decided not to try and satisfy any tastes. So, some of my choices were rounds of cheese that weighed ten kilos, twenty-pound sacks of rice, and large squares of the best butter I have ever tasted, plus scores of Portuguese sausages, all local. To fill 2 one-hundred-pound barrels on deck, I purchased potatoes and onions. Bread and jam, the Brits told, was a must for tea-time. Coffee, bread, and sherry for cooking, plus several spices overloaded a tired old truck that delivered to the ship that day.

The buying went easier than I suspected, save for the man who wouldn't stop insisting I buy the Velveeta cheese and Campbell soups they stocked for Americans. The ship sailed with all the food stores, and as I was not an open sea sailor, I flew home, then joined the voyage in Antigua.

When I stepped on board, my first question was, how did the food go? The captain said the passengers loved the fresh sausages, at first. But when they were hung in the bilge to dry, their strong reek permeated the ship, and the passengers hated them. Toward the end of the voyage most people got used to the smell and ate them like jerky, especially the men. We ran out of jam, the captain sternly remarked, and the cook drank the sherry the first day.

Rice Pilaf

Since the cook became useless on the voyage a pair of stewardesses (as they were then referred) joyously took over the cooking. And with sacks of rice on board, I heard they made a great pilaf. This is my version.

Ingredients

1 cup of white long grained rice
olive oil
1 stalk of celery, chopped fine
1 small onion, chopped fine
1 teaspoon of dried oregano
¼ cup chopped dates
¼ teaspoon cayenne
salt
2 cups chicken broth
½ cup chopped parsley
½ cup toasted pine nuts

1.   In oil brown rice until golden. Then add celery, onions, oregano, dates, cayenne, and salt.

2.   Add chicken broth and cook until dry.

3.   Stir in the parsley and pine nuts before serving

Note: Many recipes don't add in the nuts and parsley after doneness, but it makes the rice much fresher tasting.

A Moroccan Tea

As passengers on a 165-foot square-rigger, we got used to people waving to us from other boats as well as receiving lively receptions when sailing into harbors. It was the late 1970s and barefoot cruises were popular. The 1906 Regina Maris and her name drew a great deal of attention at sea, but especially when her ten thousand square feet of sail billowed in the wind. There really wasn't much wind the day we sailed into Casablanca, but our British captain said he loved to show her off with all "her sheets up." Save the cook and engineer, he would put the 18 crewmembers to work unfurling her sails.

After making the crossing from Gibraltar to North Africa we had another kind of reception in this port. A pilot boat came to meet us and guide the Regina Maris through their busy harbor. It is dramatically different entering a foreign country by private ship, especially when the vessel is a square-rigger, sheathed in copper from waterline to ballast with sides of 12-inch oak. Our pilot maneuvered us about, avoiding small craft until the captain was allowed to drop anchor. We eventually disembarked after much bureaucratic discourse and passport reviews.

It turned out the man who piloted the small vessel that led us into the port of Casablanca had notified his wife, who was sister to the king of Morocco.

This sounded exotic to us Americans and proved even more. The pilot's wife arrived remarkably soon after we anchored, toured the vessel with enthusiasm and came with an invitation. It seems the monarch's brother admired clipper ships and offered us a reception at his residence the next evening.

The following day at dusk, 8 of us arrived at a princely domain; 4 passengers, 4 crew. We stepped into a large round entry 2 stories high. Looking up, the view was of an intricately carved dome, typical of Moroccan craftsmen who carve stone to resemble lace. The entrance featured a short corridor on each side that led to rooms of identical size. One for guests, one for wives. I craned my neck to stare into the harem and saw round, veiled women dressed in black, giggling and staring back.

We were ushered into the receiving room then assembled into a line to be received by the king's brother to pay our respects. The sovereign brother asked only for the owner of the barkentine and directed his questions to him alone. The rest of us were not addressed. He would not make eye contact with the two women of the crew. He sat in a chair that resembled a throne that was placed on a platform. His casual suit was covered with a caftan. His hostess and translator was his sister, and wife of the pilot. She arranged the gathering and too was never addressed. After parading before the king, she had us sit on pillows that lined a room of about thirty feet square. Once we were settled in a large circle, his sister knelt in the middle of the room and clapped her hands. A boy of about 10 years of age rushed in and bowed. His head was wrapped turban-style, his shabby clothes out of an Arabian Nights movie. He took his commands seriously then exited from the room, never showing his back. He soon returned struggling with a large silver tray, laden with Arabic tea accoutrements that he set on the floor before the pilot's wife. Again, he exited from the room backwards. We were later told this young boy had been purchased from the streets as an infant to be owned by the master of the house and kept in servitude for his lifetime.

The tray held a bowl with a large quantity of fresh mint leaves which the sister stuffed into a silver teapot followed by many sugar cubes. Next, she reached for the pitcher of hot water. She held her pouring arm as high as possible to fill the tea pot, producing a thin stream of steaming water to cover the mint leaves. She took a large bowl of white cookies about the size of a thumb from the tray and had them passed around.

The tea was cloyingly sweet and beyond drinking for those of us who hadn't grown up with the taste. The cookies were flavorless and rock-hard. All I could think of was the boy who was barely able to manage carrying the heavy tray into the room, and what would have happened if he had faltered. I decided our medieval tea and reception with a monarch was an experience that ran uncomfortably against our American grain.

My Favorite Shortbread

I think the cookies served were to emulate shortbread, a biscuit (as the Brits would say) from colonial days. They lacked both butter and sugar. This recipe is from the talented pastry chef at Stars, the famous San Francisco restaurant with the glorious chef and owner, Jeremiah Tower. I make the shortbread stars in this book every Christmas.

Ingredients

2 sticks of sweet butter
½ cup sugar
2 cups of flour
pinch of salt

1.   Combine the butter and sugar using a standing mixer with the paddle attachment.

2.   Add the flour and salt and mix for 4 to 6 minutes.

3.   Place dough on lightly floured board and roll to ¼ inch thickness. Cut into your favorite shapes (I always use star cutters). and place on cookie sheets lined with parchment and chill for one hour.

4.   Bake at 250 degrees for about 45 minutes.

Elevator Restaurant Talk

I stepped into the elevator at the Park Plaza in New York in the eighties. A tall man and I exchanged a polite smile. An Asian woman dressed from head to toe in Gucci attire avoided eye contact with either of us. The elevator raised several stories, then lurched and came to a stop. We waited for a few minutes when a voice on the speaker said we were stuck between two floors, and it would take time to get us out. The Asian woman's face turned to stone. She pushed her back against the wall, slid to the floor, sat on her Gucci heels, and buried her head into her Gucci purse. For the forty-five-minutes we were stuck in the elevator, she seemed to put herself in a dream state. The gentleman and I struck up a conversation. He visited New York one week out of every month on business, so I asked him for a restaurant referral for our dinner that evening. We learned we were both from a suburb of L.A., and foodies. For the duration of our suspended state, we exchanged where to eat out, from dives to fine dining places. When we were finally rescued, it was with a ladder as we indeed were stuck between two floors. The moment the ladder was lowered, the Asian lady came frenetically to life. She pushed me aside and climbed out clinging to her Gucci satchel as she ascended the ladder. I said goodbye and thanked the man for our chat and climbed my way out next.

That night my husband and I had a memorable paella at a fine Spanish restaurant referred to by my fellow elevator companion. When I had finished my lovely Sherry Fino, and my husband his flan, the waiter arrived to tell us our bill had been taken care of. I looked around to see my elevator companion in the corner of the restaurant twirling his napkin above his head and smiling.

Caribbean Paella

This recipe is a mix of Caribbean and Spanish rice dishes. I loved it but can't remember where I ate it, just that it was somewhere on an island in the Netherlands Antilles.

Ingredients

1 cup short grain rice
oil for sautéing the rice
salt and pepper
 1 onion, chopped fine
2 cloves of garlic, chopped fine
3 cups of broth
handful of green pitted olives
¼ cup sultana raisins
¼ cup almonds (skinless)
¼ cup pimento sliced
cilantro for garnish

1.   Sauté rice in oil until golden, add onions and garlic plus salt and pepper

2.   When all the ingredients are hot, add broth

3.   Simmer uncovered until about half of the broth is absorbed, then add the balance of ingredients (not the cilantro).

4.   Garnish with cilantro.

Note: This rice cooks quickly because you sauté it in the beginning. The Caribs like their food exotic.

Waiters

Chef John Sedlar created some of the finest restaurants where I have ever dined, and one of my favorites was Bikini in Santa Monica, California. A waterfall quietly fluttered down a wall in this modern space with an inviting patio that drew cigar smokers after dinner (in the eighties when they were in favor). The minimalist environment of glass walls and stone floors were beautiful appointments. The attentive wait staff were never obsequious. My husband and I had finished a marvelous Asian and Latin fusion of tastes when our waitperson, as they were beginning to be called, asked us if we cared for dessert. My husband's penchant for sweets led him to spy an exotic chocolate concoction.

John, always with a sense of humor about food, had an amusing sign in the window discretely painted in gold that said Chateau d' Yaquim on tap. That was tantamount to saying, "caviar hamburgers served here." I had always liked the story, or myth, about that dessert wine. It told of the lord of the castle who soldiered off to war never dreaming that his vineyards would be neglected. His serfs were accustomed to only their master giving the order to pick his grapes and make wine, so in his absence grapes were simply not harvested. The lord was enraged upon his return to see the overripe grapes languishing on the vines. His fury provoked him to call out, "Make wine!" And today we have sautérnes . . . the finest being Chateau d' Yaquim.

As I prefer an occasional sweet wine after dinner, I ordered the storied sautérne. When the waiter set our dessert selections before us, he reversed our orders. I said, pointing to my husband's exotic dessert. "You, chauvinist pig. You assumed that I ordered this, didn't you? Meet me on the patio with my sautérne and a cigar!"

He was a gay man and that made my comments all the more amusing. I noticed him giggle all the way back to the kitchen, I felt sure to repeat my words to the staff.

Green Tomato and Green Chile Soup

This recipe is from John Sedlar's book, Modern Southwest Cuisine - a book of magnificent photos and delectable recipes. John is often referred to as "the father of Southwest Cuisine," and justifiably so.

Ingredients

7 tablespoons unsalted butter

2 medium-sized russet potatoes, peeled and cut in ¼ inch dice

2 medium onions, coarsely chopped

1 fresh Anaheim chile, stemmed seeded and coarsely chopped

1 bay leaf

1 teaspoon dried thyme

1 dozen medium-sized tomatoes, coarsely chopped

1 cup chicken broth

1 teaspoon salt

1 teaspoon white pepper

6 small sprigs fresh dill, for garnish

1.   Melt 4 tablespoons butter in a medium saucepan over moderate heat Add potatoes and sauté for 5 minutes; add onions, chile, bay leaf and thyme and sauté about 2 minutes more.

2.   Add tomatoes and chicken stock. Bring to a boil and reduce to a simmer uncovered until the vegetables are tender.

3.   Remove the bay leaf from the pan and transfer the contents to a food processor and puree. Return the puree to the saucepan and add the half and half, salt, pepper, and the remaining butter. Stir the soup and serve it in a heated bowl garnished with springs of fresh dill.

Note: John is French trained, as the recipe shows. Do make this soup, your guests will rave.

Boonie Liked Lamb

I arrived home with a leg of lamb from the market for my dinner party. I unwrapped it and let it sit on the kitchen counter. Our big orange feline, Boonie, who we named after a distant relative, Daniel Boone, sat below that counter. I didn't know he could smell the meat when it was cold but that showed how little I knew. Bringing a big piece of meat to room temperature is always best before roasting. My dinner plans were ambitious, as I had invited a noted chef to dine.

Once the meat was in the oven, Boonie laid down on the kitchen floor below the oven. His head rose from time to time to follow whiffs of roasting lamb. I always reserved a few small pieces for him. Lamb was his favorite.

Before our guests sat down to a creamy leek and onion soup, I removed the lamb from the oven to rest before carving. Boonie wove through my legs with a tall tail, politely mewing for lamb, now!

"It's too hot Boonie," I whispered, as I removed the leg to my carving board. Boonie collapsed to the floor with resignation. I returned to the dining room to remove our soup plates, and serve my composed salad of poached pears, walnuts, and blue cheese. Boonie's tail was now striking the floor with the beat of a drum. I stepped over him to carve the slightly pink meat, pleased with its perfect doneness. To the approval of all, I entered the dining room with lamb laden dinner plates and roasted vegetables. I didn't see Boonie this time. One more trip to the kitchen with a warm boat of the au jus, and I knew my dinner party was a success. We lingered at the table as guests do after enjoying a good meal. I was reaching for a dessert wine when I heard a loud thump on the floor. "Oh no, I forgot Boonie's lamb," I bellowed.

Roasted Leg of Lamb

When I first began roasting leg of lamb it was with the bone, now a bone-in leg of lamb must be special ordered. Today in my area a leg of lamb is found in the meat case, wrapped in a net, no bone. Today, I remove it from the netting and broil or barbecue it like a large steak.

Ingredients

1 leg of lamb deboned and removed from the netting

2 tablespoons of dried rosemary

1 tablespoon of dried thyme

6 cloves of garlic

juice of one lemon

olive oil

salt and pepper

1.   Flatten the leg and with a sharp knife, open the thick parts like a book (a meat cutter can do this for you).

2.   Place all the seasonings and enough oil in a small blender or coffee grinder to create a marinade and rub the mixture on the flattened side of the leg.

3.   Place the lamb on a hot grill or under an oven broiler. Turn the meat no more than once, and regularly check the temperature with a meat thermometer.

Note: Because the flattened meat is somewhat uneven, when you carve it, the slices will be well done, medium and medium rare to please all your diners. Don't be intimidated by this recipe, it is easy to cook with great results.

Jasmine Sits at Attention

After I attended chef school, I became most interested in French technique, taught their methods in my cooking school, and continue to use them today. Although I cook few French recipes, I always use their rules. I never felt we were taught enough French technique in chef school, but then I went to UCLA for my chef training, not France.

Cooking came easy to me, and I performed most methods quickly. Yet I was stopped dead in my cooking tracks when faced with making a proper French omelet. It frustrated me not to be able to make this seemingly easy egg preparation.

But I had to submit to the fact that only occasionally could I produce a yellow, properly plated omelet that was soft on the inside, not runny, and most important, without a brown exterior.

I finally decided to practice on weekends going through many eggs in the process. The mistakes had to go somewhere, and that meant Jasmine, my Chow Chow, who became my most avid omelet eater. She would hear an egg crack and come trotting to my side, sitting, watching, and waiting. There probably isn't a dog that doesn't like eggs, but Jasmine learned to adore them. She wolfed omelets with chives beaten into them, omelets filled with cheese, vegetables, even jam.

Eventually I decided I had given enough time and practice to my execution of the perfect omelet when I heard a French chef say–the only way you can make a good omelet is if you prepare them daily. I too learned that it was the measure by which a chef is usually hired in France. Now occasionally I make a great French omelet, but only occasionally.

Some years passed, and Jasmine became arthritic, a little deaf and suffered cataracts. I was in the kitchen preparing a meatloaf for my grandkids one afternoon when I cracked a couple of eggs to add to the meat mixture. Jasmine raised her head, cocked an ear toward the kitchen and stood. With some difficulty, she hobbled to my side, sat, watched, and waited.

Well, of course I stopped what I was doing and made her an omelet.

Classic French Omelet

A classic French omelet is difficult to prepare and takes skill.

Ingredients

1 medium sized skillet (a nonstick is best)

3 to 4 tablespoons of butter

3 eggs well beaten (adding the herbs below is optional but not necessary)

2 to 4 tablespoons fresh herbs, chopped fine

1.   In a medium hot skillet, melt butter and add eggs well beaten with herbs.

2.   After about a minute stir with a fork, shaking the pan at the same time. The object is to let the raw eggs move below the cooked one.

3.   When the eggs are nearly done, tilt the skillet up to force the eggs to the downside of the

skillet then fold the top of the pan's eggs (one third) to the middle.

4.   Now tap the handle so the thick part of the omelet will fall onto the last third of the omelet, then release and slip it out of the pan onto a serving plate.

Note: This is not easy to explain as it is so visual. Go to YouTube and see Jacque Pepin execute French omelets with aplomb.

Thanksgiving with the Brits

One of my daughters often brought home a visiting Brit from across the pond. She always seemed comfortable with their banter and humor. One Thanksgiving, in her early twenties, she called to ask if it was okay to bring two lads for Thanksgiving dinner.

"Well, of course," I said.

She added, "And don't dress-up too much, these guys come from a humble background, maybe wear your dots. You know how the Brits like dots."

She meant my older top and pants of polka dots.

The lads arrived with a bouquet that looked like it had been plucked from someone's garden. Polite and respectful, the young boys appeared very pleased to be accepted into our home for our traditional turkey fare. Both of them wanted to help and were most curious about what I was cooking. When I basted the turkey, its size brought wide eyes and delightful grins. A modern Charles Dickens story came to mind. They especially loved the tastes of the tart cranberries. They asked why the stuffing was baked outside the bird. My daughter took me aside and explained that her friends had barely scraped their airfare together and were thrilled to be our guests. She said they liked me a lot, and thought I looked younger than the mothers of grown children in England.

"And you wore your dots," she added. I smiled and hiked up my older capris. It was time for more basting. We had a rhythm going. One lad held the oven door open while the other pulled the turkey forward for me to baste. It was this last turkey basting that my polka dotted pants dropped from my waist and settled at my ankles.

One Brit went running into the living room, calling, "Your Mums lost her knickers!"

Fortunately, it was a time when women wore pantyhose. But to this day a Thanksgiving dinner does not pass without someone recounting this story.

Cranberry Relish

This exceptionally easy condiment lends relief to the richness of the Thanksgiving dinner.

Ingredients

1 package of cranberries, washed and picked over

1 orange, well washed unpeeled and cut into eighths with seeds removed

1 apple, well washed with the core removed and cut into eights

1 inch piece of peeled ginger, cut into small pieces

⅓ cup sugar

pinch of salt

1.   Start the processor and drop the ginger down the feeding tube until well ground. Remove the top of the processor and add balance of ingredients and process until you have a mash.

Note: Best made a day ahead.

The Best Food Compliment Ever

When my twin grandchildren were about five years old in the early two thousands, they discovered pizza, and like most kids loved it immediately. I told them I could make them pizza pies, which brought giggles. They didn't believe me until I brought dough home from Trader Joe's. I knew having a head start on the project was a good idea. I portioned out pieces of dough in golf-ball sizes for them, and a large one for me. Together we made our dough into rounds. They worked their pieces until they were dirty little circles and inedible, but we all had fun. Flour covered their hands and arms. Noses too. After washing up, we moved to the liquefier to puree tomatoes. Together, we placed them in a pan to simmer on the stove. They stood on stools to season, stir, and stir some more while they watched the sauce change color from red to orange. We tasted it over and over until we all agreed it was perfect. It wasn't easy waiting for the sauce to cool, so during that time we pulled our large ball of mozzarella cheese into small pieces. We picked basil leaves from their stems. Afterwards our fingers smelled like the green leaves but didn't taste so good. Next, I showed them how to put the dough on the wooden peel so we could safely slip it into the hot oven, and a new word was learned. Finally, I said it was time to dress the pie, which drew more giggles. As we stared at the red, white, and green color of the toppings, I explained that we had made a Margherita Pizza. It was difficult waiting the long ten minutes while the pizza cooked. They watched me cut the pizza into triangles and serve them. Finally, after blowing on them for a while, they munched them up with greedy appetites. When I asked if it was worth the wait, I got affirmative nods.

A few weeks passed, and Rex, the boy twin, was invited to a birthday party of a five-year-old that was held at Chuck E. Cheese Pizza. He came up to me and said, "DoDo, can you come to the party and make the pizza?"

French Bread Pizza

I was never a fan of pizza with a heavy base of tomato sauce topped with cheese, but soon became enamored by Wolfgang Puck's pizzas. I learned he doesn't incorporate tomatoes into his pizzas. I adapted a faux pizza using a baguette for easy cooking.

Ingredients

olive oil for sautéing
1 medium sized, yellow zucchini cubed
1 medium sized, green zucchini cubed
1 bell pepper cubed
1 tablespoon garlic salt
1 tablespoon dried oregano
3 tablespoons of balsamic or sherry vinegar
¼ cup fontina grated
¼ cup mozzarella
¼ cup parmesan, grated

1.   Sauté the above vegetables with garlic salt and oregano and when al dente, remove from heat. Add vinegar and mix in the cheeses.

2.   Place mixture in baguette with some of the bread removed.

3.   Place under the broiler and remove when bubbling.

Note: Cut the baguette in half down the middle before halving it horizontally.

A Different Kind of Marshmallow

Nikki, my twelve-year-old granddaughter, and I share our like for a good marshmallow, so the other day when I found wonderfully hand-made ones at a gift shop, I bought two packages. As a retired chef, there are simply some things I no longer make, and this sticky confection is one of them.

I'm pleased that my twin grandkids eat most food. They have grown up with me not only cooking a variety of foods, but a variety of cuisines as well.

"Nikki," I said, "I found some great marshmallows, want one?"

"Sure, Dodo," she said, using my diminutive name from my childhood.

I wiped up my cutting board, unpackaged the large white puffs and cut one in half, handing it to her. "Aren't they good, Nikki?"

She nodded but as I left the room, she asked, "Dodo, what did you use your knife for before you cut the marshmallow?"

I stopped to think for a moment.

Before I could answer, she said. "Was it a jalapeno, Dodo?"

"As a matter of fact, it was, Nikki," I replied. "Would you like another marshmallow not tainted with the taste of chili?"

"No, it's actually kind of interesting," Nikki said. "I like it!"

I include marshmallows when serving a fondue as a dessert dipped in ganache (recipe on page 54 with the 'Ants' story).

Let's Make Mole

Rex, my grandson, is a great help in the kitchen. When he was twelve years old, I asked him if he wanted to help me make mole. Silently, he nodded. (Rex speaks only when necessary).

I said I would do the mis en plaze for him and explained that phrase (in French) defines the prep work for a recipe, especially one as complex as mole. I had a simmering pot on the stove with a pork shoulder, or a small turkey, I can't remember which. The brewing broth also contained a bouquet garni (bundle of herbs) and mirepoix (2 parts onions, one-part carrots and celery). I think he liked the explanations of the ingredients and registered them, but with his limited words, you never really knew.

I seeded and removed the veins of Mulato, Ancho and Pasilla chilies then roasted and simmered them. I had Rex count out 24 peanuts, 24 raisons, 24 almonds and 1 tablespoon of sesame seeds. I roasted them over a comal, a flat round of cast iron.

I briefly sautéed dried anise, fresh thyme, bay leaf and marjoram. I removed the skin from one tomato, chopped it plus an onion and three cloves of garlic, which I also sautéed.

"Okay, Rex let's make mole."

He set up the blender to begin. As per my instruction, he pureed the chilies. I added just enough meat broth, then sautéed nuts, seeds and raisins and added them to the chili puree. Finally, the tomato, onion, and garlic, again adjusting the liquid.

"Smells good Dodo. Are we finished?"

164

"Not yet. Now we remove it to a pan and simmer it for a half hour. Please set a timer."

He picked up his phone to set the timer, then played a game on it.

When the simmer time was up, I said, "Rex, put a little mole into our small blender, and add this Mexican chocolate I have grated, and this half a banana."

"Really?" he asked.

"Really," I said. Then I asked him to return this mixture to the mole pot and instructed him to stir.

Dipping a rolled warm tortilla into the muddy, brick colored sauce, he said, "Boy this is good, Dodo."

That evening invited guests and family raved over the mole.

"Who made this?" someone asked.

Rex raised his hand and said, "I did."

Mexico City Mole

Authentic mole is both a daunting task and a labor of love for the dedicated cook. This particular mole is made in the style of Mexico City. It is more complex and cosmopolitan in style rather than rural. The recipe includes a series of steps, almost like the French execute in many of their recipes. Perhaps that is due to the short rule of Maximillian and Carlotta.

Note: Start this recipe with a pot of simmering pork, chicken, or turkey on the stove as you will use the broth to liquefy the following ingredients using several steps.

Ingredients

several tablespoons of oil for sautéing
6 to 7 dried mulato chiles, seeds and veins removed
6 to 7 dried ancho chiles, seeds and veins removed

3 dried pasilla chiles, seeds and veins removed

1.   Quickly fry the above ingredients in a minimum amount of oil and drain. Then simmer in water for about 5 to 10 minutes. Using a strong blender, puree the chiles using the simmering water to get a runny puree.

20 to 24 peanuts
4 tablespoons raisins
20 to 24 almonds
1 tablespoon sesame seeds
salt

1.   Quickly fry the above, add to the chili mixture and puree in the blender, using enough broth on the stove to keep the mixture a loose puree.

1 tablespoon anise seeds
1 teaspoon dried thyme

2 bay leaves

1 tablespoon dried marjoram

1.   Quickly fry the above ingredients, drain, and remove bay leaves. Add these to the blender and puree, using broth on the stove.

1 tomato, skin removed and chopped

1 white onion, coarsely chopped

4 cloves of garlic, coarsely chopped

salt to taste

1.   Sauté the above ingredients until the onions are golden, then add to the nearly completed mole. The consistency of the mole should be like a medium thick gravy.

Note: The reason for sautéing the groups of items is to release flavor. The French taught us this trick, as simmering alone will not do so.

2.   Remove the mole to a pot and simmer for about 20 minutes, after which you can adjust the mole thickness with broth. The mole will thicken during cooking. Taste the mixture and add salt to taste.

½ of a ripe banana, mashed

½ ounce of Mexican chocolate (this is chocolate made with cinnamon and sugar)

1.   Melt the chocolate and add the mashed banana into the chocolate and mix well. Add to mole and mix well. Turn off the heat - YOU HAVE MOLE!

Note: If desired, the simmering pork or poultry can be added to the mole at this time.

Grandkids and a Tasting

When my twin grandkids were toddlers, near the turn of the last century, they crawled up on high stools at my kitchen-bar-counter where I held a nearly omnipotent position. For those short years, I was their television and personal chef. I would cook. They would taste, and best of all they got to choose their favorite preparations.

I lovingly called them "The Brats."

One cooking session, the girl-twin said, "Umm tastes lemony, Dodo. I like it."

Ah ha, I saw an opportunity.

"We are going to have a tasting," I said. The twins wiggled and grew serious as I put out tiny capfuls of vinegars: malt, red wine, cider, champagne, and balsamic. I explained these were strong tastes and to just touch their finger to the liquids, then to their tongue. Of course, we had glasses of water for cleansing their palates between tastes. They proceeded with serious interest.

Rex chose the red wine vinegar, validating the French's belief that men have stronger palates than women. Nikki chose the malt vinegar, validating that woman prefer carbs in any form.

These experiments moved into other areas. One afternoon for our lunch, we pan seared sand dabs together. The Brats help me carefully lower the fish into the skillet of bubbling butter. With fascination, they watched me turn them and then place them on a long platter. Nikki's eyes grew wide when I filleted them. She drew out the bones, "booones." With confidence and a far more sober expression, Rex shook his head.

"A skeleton," he announced.

Then there was the time I made them a Lyonnaise salad, appropriately topped with a poached egg and bits of sautéed bacon. Nikki loved poking into the yolk of the egg as it ran over the greens.

"It's such a great sauce," she hummed. And that's how they became entrenched foodies, with no turning back.

Lyonnaise Salad for Four

Ingredients

4 cups of Friése greens
2 tablespoons extra virgin olive oil
4 strips of bacon, chopped fine
1 shallot, chopped fine
2 to 4 tablespoons sherry vinegar
1 tablespoon Dijon mustard
salt
cracked pepper

1. Sauté bacon until almost crisp. Remove and drain the skillet a little. Whisk into the skillet olive oil, shallots, sherry vinegar, Dijon mustard, and pinch of salt for the dressing. Set aside.

2. Poach 4 eggs no longer than 3 minutes. Divide the greens onto four plates and top each plate with the eggs and bacon. Rewarm the

dressing and pour over each egg. Crack black pepper on top.

Carnitas

Early Sunday morning, I stared into the refrigerator that was crowded with large foil containers of Mexican food, wondering why? Then I remembered that two fathers had taken teenagers to the UCLA football game last night. The over-zealous dads had ordered too much food. I would have to incorporate these leftovers into several meals and share the balance with some neighbors, too. Then of course there were the dogs. And that reminded me of the ravens.

For some years I have been feeding ravens. They usually get scraps of old bread and pastry items. Yet watching a television special about these birds the other evening, the ones that nest at the Tower of London, I watched a keeper feed them the sheep hearts. He explained it was their favorite food.

With that in mind, I went to the drawer where I keep gloves for certain food preparations and slipped one on. I reached into the container of carnitas (shredded cooked pork) and grabbed a generous handful. Down my steps and across the street I went, calling the ravens.

"Regina! Reginald!"

I placed the meat on a large flat stone where they usually swoop down, expecting their morning offerings. I always spread their scraps across the stone or greedy Reginald will stand over the food and not let Regina eat.

This morning, Reginald went wild over the carnitas, running back and forth trying to dominate the spread of meat. She, cleverer than he, quickly filled her beak and fluttered a few feet away to enjoy her faire. He was infuriated that she absconded with some of his meat. He lost all composure and appeared senseless for a few moments. Outraged, he finally got hold of himself and followed suit, and practiced her technique.

Carnitas

Ingredients

1 pork butt (shoulder of the pig)

1 onion

6 cloves of garlic

2 Tablespoons salt

3 cloves

1 stick of cinnamon

1 tablespoon dried oregano

½ cup milk

salt

1.   Cover the pork butt in water and add all the ingredients, (you can cube the meat but use the bone, as it lends flavor).

2.   Bring to a boil, then to a simmer and cook uncovered until the meat falls off the bone (at least an hour). Skim off the gray foam that surfaces.

Remove the pork to a cutting board and shred it with forks.

3.   Add meat to a skillet and on low heat add milk until it absorbs. Add salt to taste.

Note: Some people add a few dried chilies to the simmering pork, some add an orange, carrots, celery and so on. However, this meat needs little embellishments.

Twins Learn Dinner Talk

When my twin grandkids, Rex, and Nikki, had learned most of their etiquette skills at the dinner table, I explained that dinner conversation was a skill, too. That led to interesting topics to unfold during our dining sessions. One evening it steered them into discussing my age as we shared a shrimp cocktail.

We occasionally ate at a fine dining restaurant, and on one of those evenings an elderly woman entered. She pushed her way toward her table with a noisy walker and with each step she raised and banged her walker down hard on the carpet. As she plodded toward her seat, there was something of an attitude in her harsh stride that said, I'm here and get out of my way. She was difficult not to stare at. Ten-year-old Rex found it hardest to divert his eyes. I had to remind him that it was rude to keep watching her.

"One day, I may be that old and have to use a walker, too, Rex."

His twin, Nikki, nodded and turned away with understanding.

Rex shook his head firmly and said, "You'll never be like that."

I was hoping he meant I would never have her sour attitude, not reach her age. I tried to move the topic on.

"You kids are in elementary school now, and I am getting older. Am I going to see you move on to middle school?"

Both displayed strong nods.

"What about high school and college? Am I going to see you graduate from there, too?"

"Yep," Nikki said. Rex affirmed her comment with another nod.

"And what about marriage? Am I going to see you two marry and have kids?"

"Noooo, you'll be dead by then," Rex said.

Shrimp Cocktail

It's common to buy a shrimp cocktail sauce but try this one. I first enjoyed this sauce years ago in Vera Cruz Mexico. It is a fascinating city to dine and serves exciting fusion-style dishes.

Ingredients

8 cooked shrimp, reserve one shrimp (poach only until they are pink)

½ cup catsup

½ cup cilantro greens

l tablespoon Tabasco sauce (or your favorite red hot sauce)

1 tablespoon brown sugar

¼ cup lime juice

2 stalks celery coarsely chopped

salt to taste

1.	Place the one reserved shrimp and all the other ingredients in a liquefier and thoroughly blend until smooth. Taste, and if needed adjust flavor with sugar and lime juice.

Note: The added shrimp to the sauce lends flavor and a little thickness.

Middle Eastern Dive

When my twin grandkids were about twelve, I explained that I planned to have a party to celebrate publishing my novel. As my story is set in 1400 BC Egypt, I wanted to cook foods for my guests that the ancient people of that period ate. Would they want to taste that food at a restaurant in town called Dahab with me? They seemed modestly interested. With their parents, they were becoming able travelers and adventurous eaters. So, I got a reserved affirmative from them to join me.

"How far away is the restaurant?" the boy asked, "and how long will we have to wait for our food?"

"We'll get our food quickly," I said, avoiding mentioning the amount of time it would take to get to the other side of town. I added that we would be going to a rather humble place. The word humble needed defining to my privileged Brats.

"This little eatery," describing it the best I could, "is a bit of a dive, and it changes into a hookah parlor at night."

"What's that?" they exclaimed. After an explanation of the Middle Eastern practice of smoking and the accoutrements, they were now genuinely interested. When we arrived, we had to walk through a patio where lone smokers were drawing hard on their pipes, followed by exhaling huge billows of smoke. The kids walked slowly through this area. When we got seated, the oil cloth on the table was a little greasy and the floor a little gritty. But the kids didn't notice. They were craning their necks to see the patio smokers. A tall man with a bushy black beard took our order, which arrived promptly. We dined on kababs, hummus, baba ghanoush, labneh, a Fattoush salad and a Bousa cake. When the table was set with the various foods, it looked like a feast, and the kids dug in with enthusiasm.

"Umm, this is good, Dodo, I want another kabab," Rex said.

"And I want more too, Grandma!" Nikki said.

We all ate to our contentment and when we returned home, they had a story to beguile their parents. After that, the kids really took to Middle Eastern food and complained vigorously how the same food they got locally was never as good as Dahab's.

My House Hummus

This hummus has a few twists that make it even more delicious.

Ingredients

1 can of 15 to 16 ounces of drained garbanzo beans (take the time to remove the skins)

liquid from the can of garbanzo beans

4 cloves of garlic (take the time to poach the garlic for 60 seconds in simmering water)

3 or 4 tablespoons of tahini

juice of one lemon

¼ cup or more of olive oil

salt to taste

1.   Start your food processor and drop the garlic down the feeding tube until it is finely chopped. Turn off the processor and add the garbanzo beans and liquid, the tahini, the lemon juice, and salt. Pulse until roughly incorporated. If it is too thick add more garbanzo bean liquid.

2.   With the processor on full speed slowly drizzle olive oil down the tube until the hummus is very smooth.

Note: Poaching the garlic ahead softens its sharpness and removing the garbanzo bean skins lends great smoothness.

Christmas, Dogs, and Chardonnay

It was Christmas. My son, his wife, along with their boy and girl twins, were away traveling. My older daughter lives in New York, so I knew my youngest, Juliet, was feeling rather blue about no place to gather for the holidays. After all, we're a cooking family who all participate in the preparation of a festive Christmas meal, which was not to happen this year. I mentioned to Juliet that Wolfgang Puck had taken over the food service for the hotel Bel Air and we could spend a few days there. She perked up and we made reservations.

Because we are a family of foodies, I was happy that Juliet seemed pleased with my suggestion to stay and dine at this little-known hideaway. I made this our gifts to one another. I think I speak for most foodies when I say that an inviting food environment rates high. In the garden room where we took most of our and our dog's meals, a huge sixty-year-old bougainvillea cascaded over the entry. For me, the Bel Air rates right up there with the pyramids. Born in Southern California, I love outdoor eating. I also appreciate casual elegance, not an easy thing to pull off without artifice. You never feel underdressed here, and friendliness among diners is unanimous.

We also love the hotel because they welcome dogs. When you arrive, awaiting your canine is his or her own enormous pillow, water, and food dishes, plus a cookie in the form of a bone, baked in Wolfgang Puck's kitchen. While standing in the garden area with her miniature Chihuahua, Juliet heard a man with a deep Welsh accent say, "My, what a lovely cable knit sweater that is on your sweet dog." It was Sir Anthony Hopkins! That night at dinner, a man was flanked at his feet by his two sleeping Vislas who never uttered a sound. And in the morning, on a long patch of grass, we made friends with owners of an exuberant fox terrier looking like he had stepped out of the movies – The Thin Man – of course.

We chose not to take our dogs to Christmas dinner but enjoyed the diners who did. Soon, a stuffy sommelier stood next to Juliet asking her if he could explain the wine list. I thought this was not a good beginning to our Christmas dinner. Stuffiness and the Bel Air do not go hand in hand. We decided he must be new. Juliet could have explained the wine list to him—well maybe just the chardonnay offerings. Not making eye contact with him, she said, "Sure."

After it was established that she drank chardonnay exclusively, the sommelier proceeded with his long-winded litany of wine facts, Chardonnay vintages, grand cru and so forth. Granted it's a popular wine with her generation and an enormous number of wine makers produce it. I'll have to admit that she has tried most of them, that is the ones she could afford. The sommelier waxed on stating bottle prices, the costs per glass, the finest vintages in the hotel cellar when he finally took a breath. Juliet said, "I'll take a glass of the cheap chardonnay."

That comment seemed to bring him down to earth.

Dog Biscuits

These home-made dog biscuits are approved by the American Kennel Club.

Ingredients

2 cups flour
1 cup canned pumpkin
½ cup peanut butter

1.   Mix all ingredients to form a dough.

2.   On a floured service roll out the dough and cut into doggie-bone shapes.

3.   Bake at 375 degrees for 12 minutes.

Chilaquiles

All countries incorporate leftover bread products into their cuisines. Who doesn't love French toast, a tasty Bruschetta or a wienerschnitzel crusted with golden breadcrumbs? In Mexico, day-old tortillas are torn apart and quickly stir fried with a salsa, leftovers and maybe a little cheese. Eggs or small pieces of meat can also be added. The variations are many, and it is best described as a deconstructed enchilada. This is fast food at its best, often a late-night favorite in the commercial kitchen where so many Hispanics labor. and enjoyed not just by the staff. Sophisticated restaurants in Mexico City would refer to chilaquiles as muy colonial.

But in the western United States, where they have become ubiquitous, we do not disparage chilaquiles. My son recently pointed out that the word now exists in spell check. I have probably served this dish to more people than any other, and for a reason not entirely clear, men of all ages can't get enough. I often cook them for Rex, my grandson, and his friends at breakfast, which brings praise like I have never received. I add egg for the breakfast meal, and when boys have spent the night, I receive the friendliest of good mornings.

Not long ago, I attended a volleyball tournament at our local gym to watch Rex play in the finals. His parents and I walked past benched young men anxious to play. When we came to his team, three of his mates immediately stood, walked to me with warm hugs.

I said, "Those are chilaquile hugs."

Chilaquiles

Ingredients

1 dozen tortillas, cubed into 1-inch squares

3 or 4 tablespoons of oil for frying

3 beaten eggs

6 ounces of green chile salsa

3 ounces of Havarti cheese (I buy it sliced and tear it into pieces)

garnish with limes and cilantro

1.   Fry the tortilla pieces in about a ¼ inch of oil. Continue moving the tortillas in the pan with thongs until they are about half crisp, half soft.

2.   Add the beaten eggs, stir in well and just before they are set, add the salsa, and incorporate well.

3.   When the chilaquiles are hot, remove from the stove and incorporate the cheese. Lightly fold in the cheese.

Note: You want the tortilla squares to be half crisp and not soggy. This takes about 5 minutes. The rest of the recipe goes fast like a stir-fry. I would double the recipe because the chilaquiles disappear once served. The finished product should be soft with the cheese just melted.

Acknowledgements

Finishing this book would not have been possible without family and friends. To my grandchildren, Nikki and Rex, thank you for serving as a constant source of inspiration. Cat Spydell, thank you for your edits, getting the manuscript off the ground and started toward completion. Mimi Swan, thank you for your eyes and astute proofreading to help solidify the book into its final form. Quincy McKay, thank you for your aesthetic cover that represents my story. Nic, my gratitude to you as always.

From Dolores Maria Davis:

My youth was permeated with good cooks of varying nationalities. I was fortunate to live in Mexico City for two years, as well as travel internationally. After raising a family, in mid-life I attended chef school at UCLA. Subsequently I created a cooking school and cooked for many private clients. I even took food assignments outside the U.S.

Then I had grandchildren, and that started another circle of food events, with many instances reflected here in Funny Food Stories.

I hope you enjoy some of the food stories from my childhood through my adult life, as well as my recipes.

Other Books by Dolores Maria Davis

Harem Twins Series

Black Angel Series

www.ingramcontent.com/pod-product-compliance
Lightning Source LLC
Chambersburg PA
CBHW061324200626
46813CB00017B/2835